FOR OLIVER AND JACK
−LM

WITH THANKS TO DR. FRED EHRLICH, M.D.,
FOR HIS CAREFUL REVIEW OF THE TEXT

Text copyright © 2007 by Harriet Ziefert, Inc.

Illustrations copyright © 2007 by Liz Murphy

All rights reserved / CIP Data is available.

Published in the United States 2007 by

🍎 Blue Apple Books

P.O. Box 1380, Maplewood, N.J. 07040

www.blueapplebooks.com

Distributed in the U.S. by Chronicle Books

First Edition

Printed in China

ISBN 13 : 978-1-59354-593-2

ISBN 10 : 1-59354-593-2

3 5 7 9 10 8 6 4 2

A B C
DOCTOR

Liz Murphy

Blue Apple Books

Doctors are busy people. If you need to see the doctor, you have to make an **appointment** before you go. In an emergency, if you are injured or very sick the doctor will see you right away.

Appointment

Bandage

Bumps and bruises can turn all kinds of colors before they get better—brown, purple, yellow . . . gross! Sometimes you wear a **bandage** to protect a bump or a cut while it heals.

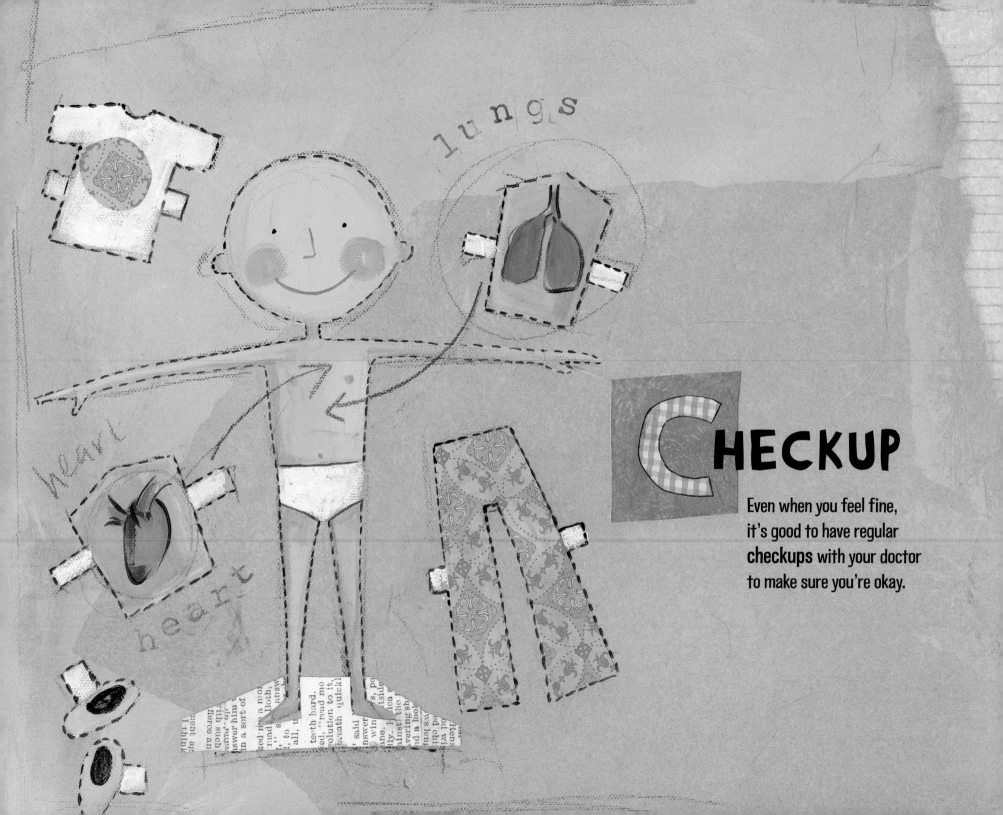

lungs

heart

heart

Checkup

Even when you feel fine, it's good to have regular **checkups** with your doctor to make sure you're okay.

Doctor

Doctors help you get better, whether it's giving you a shot, prescribing medicine, or telling you not to worry, because you'll just get better on your own.

Examination

In a regular **examination**, your doctor will listen to your heart, take your temperature, measure your height and weight, and check you all over.

FEVER

Normally, your body's temperature is about 98.6° F. If your temperature goes over 100°, you've got a **fever**. This means you are sick.

Germs

Germs are so tiny you can see them only under a microscope. There are two kinds of germs—some are called bacteria and some are called viruses. Not all germs are bad, but some can make you sick.

HAND HYGIENE

It's very important to have good **hand hygiene**, so wash your hands with soap and water often.

INOCULATION

Nobody likes getting a shot, but **inoculations** (injecting special medicine under your skin) keep you from getting serious diseases. You'll feel a tiny prick—and maybe you'll get a sticker or lollipop as a reward.

JOINT

Joints are places where your bones connect to each other, like your elbows or your knees. Try to bend all the joints in your fingers— now try your toes.

KNEE BRACE

If you hurt your knee while playing sports, or even if you just fall on your knee a certain way, you might need a **knee brace** to support your knee while it heals.

Pad pulls knee back

raised sole

brace pushes knee back.

LIGHT

During a checkup, your doctor will look into your ears and throat with a **light** to check for infections.

Sometimes **medicine** tastes good, and sometimes it tastes bad. Sometimes it's a pill and sometimes it's a syrup. It's always important to take your medicine when you're feeling sick, so that you'll get better.

MEDICINE

Nurse

A **nurse** helps the doctor during your examination by taking your height, weight, temperature, and blood pressure. Sometimes it's the nurse who gives you a shot.

OTOSCOPE

A doctor uses an **otoscope** to look into your ears. An otoscope has a light and a magnifying glass so that the doctor can see your eardrum.

PRESCRIPTION

If you're sick and there's a medicine
that will help you get better,
the doctor will give your mom or dad
a **prescription** to fill at the pharmacy.

QUESTIONS

Sometimes doctors and nurses ask a lot of **questions** so they can figure out why you're not feeling well.

If you have any **questions** for the doctor, be sure to ask.

If the doctor taps your knee with a **reflex hammer**, she's checking your reflexes. Reflexes are movements your body makes when it reacts to something. For example, when the doctor taps your knee, your lower leg will jump a little.

REFLEX HAMMER

STETHOSCOPE

Your doctor will use a **stethoscope** to listen to your heart and lungs. Sometimes you will be told to take deep breaths and sometimes to hold your breath.

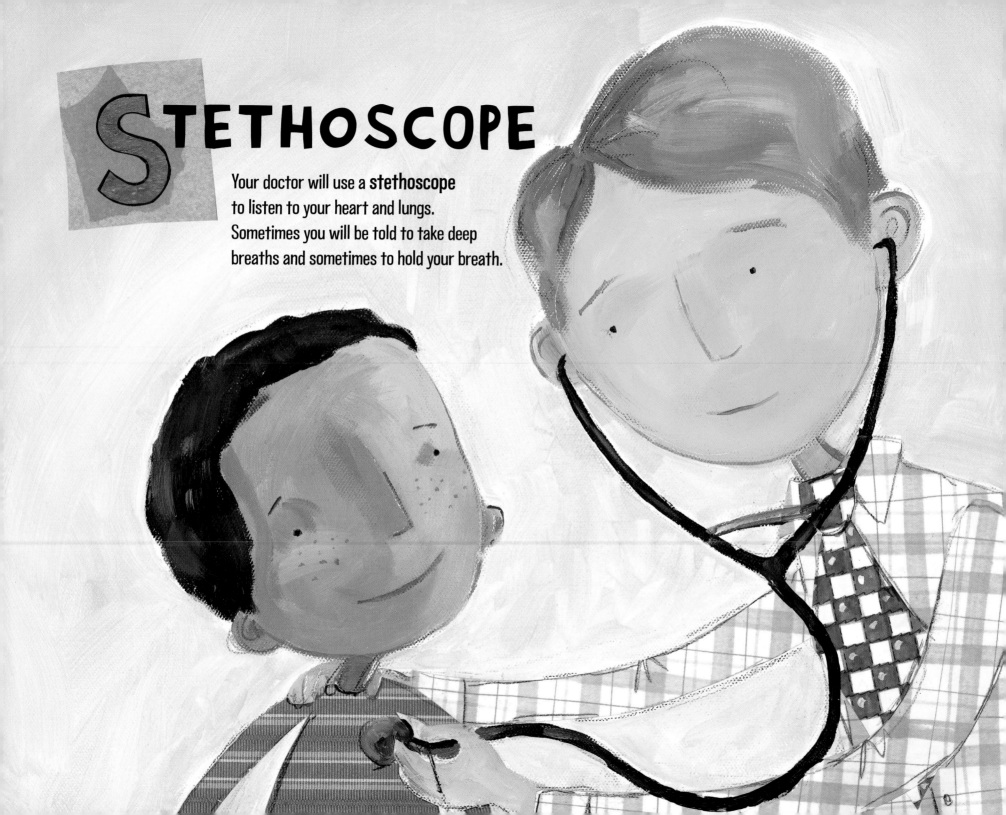

THERMOMETER

Thermometers are used to take your temperature. Thermometers used to be made of glass and were filled with a substance called mercury, but now many are digital and your temperature is taken in your ear or mouth.

Doctors sometimes ask for a **urine sample** during your checkup. They run tests on your urine to make sure your body is running well.

PLEASE PUT YOUR SAMPLE IN HERE
THANK YOU

URINE SAMPLE

Vomit

If you feel like you're going to **vomit**, you've probably got food poisoning, the stomach flu, or motion sickness. Vomiting helps get whatever is making you sick out of your system.

WHEELCHAIR

There are different kinds of **wheelchairs** for people who can't walk—wheelchairs that someone pushes from behind, wheelchairs with motors, even wheelchairs for playing sports.

X-RAY

x-ray

X-rays take pictures of your bones. If you hurt your ankle, the doctor will probably take an X-ray to make sure none of your ankle bones are broken.

YUCKY

There's no reason to keep feeling **yucky**
when all you have to do is see the doctor to feel . . .

A ZILLION TIMES BETTER!